21st
Century
Skills Library

GLOBAL PRODUCTS

GASOLINE

Kevin Cunningham

Cherry Lake Publishing
Ann Arbor, Michigan

CHERRY LAKE
Publishing

Published in the United States of America by Cherry Lake Publishing
Ann Arbor, Michigan
www.cherrylakepublishing.com

Content Adviser: Shari Dunn-Norman, PhD, Associate Professor, Petroleum
Engineering, University of Missouri-Rolla, Rolla, Missouri

Photo Credits: Cover and page 1, © Konstantin Sutyagin, used under license from
Shutterstock, Inc.; page 4, © Pablo Paul/Alamy; page 6, © Pictorial Press Ltd./Alamy;
page 8, © Avesun, used under license from Shutterstock, Inc.; page 9, © Tselichtchev,
used under license from Shutterstock, Inc.; page 12, © Mike Abrahams/Alamy; page
13, © Peter Jordan/Alamy; page 14, © Richard Levine/Alamy; page 15, © iStockphoto.
com/urbanraven; page 17, © Adrian Arbib/Alamy; page 19, © iStockphoto.com/
northwestmedia; page 20, © Chad McDermott, used under license from Shutterstock,
Inc.; page 23, © Carmen Sedano/Alamy; page 24, © Classic Stock/Alamy; page 26, © Ted
Pink/Alamy

Map by XNR Productions Inc.

Library of Congress Cataloging-in-Publication Data
Cunningham, Kevin, 1966–
Gasoline / by Kevin Cunningham.
  p. cm.—(Global products)
ISBN-13: 978-1-60279-121-3
ISBN-10: 1-60279-121-X
1. Petroleum—Juvenile literature. 2. Gasoline—Juvenile literature.
I. Title. II. Series.
TP690.25.C86 2008
665.5'3827—dc22   2007034974

Cherry Lake Publishing would like to acknowledge the work of
The Partnership for 21st Century Skills.
Please visit www.21stcenturyskills.org *for more information.*

TABLE OF CONTENTS

CHAPTER ONE

THE GASOLINE AGE

Crude oil is poured into a beaker in a lab.

"How much gas will it take us to get to Mount Rushmore?" Matthew asked Uncle John as they drove to the gas station.

"We'll have to fill up the tank more than once," his uncle said. "The petroleum industry is going to make some good money off of us."

"Petrole . . . what? I thought we put gasoline in the car."

"Gasoline starts out as liquid petroleum," Uncle John replied. "We take the liquid petroleum out of the ground and turn it into gasoline."

"So petroleum is a kind of liquid?" Matthew asked.

"The liquid form of petroleum—what we often call crude oil—is usually what people mean when they talk about how gasoline is made," Uncle John said. "But petroleum can also be a gas instead of a liquid. You know, I think there are still a couple of wells near here. I remember them from when I started working at the refinery. Why don't we drive out and see where petroleum comes from?"

The Chinese had drilled into the earth for salt since ancient times. In the 1850s, a group of people came up with the idea that they could tap into underground deposits of "rock oil"—what we call crude oil—by using the same methods. Their idea had nothing to do with gasoline. At the time, gasoline wasn't even used. The investors wanted the petroleum to make **kerosene**, a kind of oil used to light houses in the days before electricity.

A driller named Edwin L. Drake struck petroleum at Titusville, Pennsylvania, in the summer of 1859. This kicked off history's first oil rush and started the petroleum industry as we know it. In the years that followed, John D. Rockefeller founded and expanded Standard Oil. It

John D. Rockefeller was born in 1839 and founded The Standard Oil Company in 1870.

became one of the first giant corporations. Rockefeller eventually controlled kerosene production in the United States and around the world.

Other companies, however, were able to break into the business. Royal Dutch opened up petroleum wells in what is now Indonesia. Union Oil set up shop in the state of California. Shell of Great Britain began harvesting petroleum in Russia. The Mellon family, founders of Gulf Oil, was the first to build an important **pipeline** connecting Oklahoma's oil fields to Port Arthur, Texas. Other companies included Sun Oil and the Texas Company (Texaco), both founded in 1901.

While the new petroleum companies scrambled to get a share of the kerosene market, a handful of engineers and machinists were building automobiles. These machines were powered by another petroleum product—gasoline. Before these new "motor cars" came along, petroleum companies considered gasoline mostly useless. That changed quickly.

In 1904, Oldsmobile became the first company to sell more than 5,000 automobiles (its Curved Dash model) in a single year. Soon after, Ford Motor Company's Model T hit the market and became the best-selling car in the world. Gasoline became an increasingly important product. Standard Oil sold more gasoline than kerosene for the first time in 1911.

The gasoline age had arrived. Today, petroleum is as important as any **raw material** in the world. It is essential to the economy of every nation. Keeping supplies of it flowing is often the reason for many U.S. government decisions—and those of other governments, too.

A colorful character named Columbus "Dad" Joiner made one of the biggest petroleum strikes in U.S. history. In 1927, the 67-year-old Joiner began to search for oil in East Texas with hand-me-down equipment and a small crew. Three years later, his persistence paid off. On October 3, 1930, a loud gurgling noise suddenly came out of one of Joiner's wells. Oil and water exploded into the Texas sky.

Joiner had tapped into the East Texas Field, commonly referred to as the Black Giant, a 45-mile-long (72-kilometer) petroleum reservoir. He sold his stake in the Black Giant for $1.33 million and spent the rest of his life trying, and failing, to make another big strike.

*The gasoline that is pumped into cars at gas
stations is made from crude oil.*

In the United States alone, people use about 385 million gallons
(1,457,383,537 liters) of gasoline every day. About a third of it comes from
petroleum pumped out of fields in the United States. The rest is imported
from overseas. But the gasoline we put in our cars is quite different from
the crude oil form of petroleum we take from the ground.

CHAPTER TWO

DRILLING FOR PETROLEUM

Pumpjacks are used to get oil out of the ground.

Uncle John pulled over to the side of a country road. Matthew saw a metal machine out in the field. One end was shaped like a horse's head and nodded up and down. A black box covered the opposite end.

Uncle John pointed to the machine. "That's a pumpjack," he said. "It helps pump the petroleum out of the ground."

"How did they know it was under a cornfield, though?" Matthew asked.

"People who look for petroleum use high-tech tools to scope out new deposits," Uncle John said. "Sometimes features on the ground itself indicate that petroleum is nearby. So satellite cameras are useful because they offer an overhead view of the land. Engineers and geologists direct sound waves into the earth. If the waves bounce back in certain ways, there may be crude oil below. Information collected by people is put into computers. Computer programs use that information to draw three-dimensional maps of the underground terrain. They can even draw animated maps of how petroleum moves through the rock."

"Why don't they just drill?" Matthew said.

"Well," Uncle John said, "using those tools helps a company improve its chances of hitting the oil. And that is important because a dry well—a hole with nothing it in—means a lot of lost time and money."

❋ ❋ ❋

Drilling for petroleum begins by boring into the earth from a steel tower called a derrick. One common method uses a rotating piece of metal called a **bit**. It is sort of a giant version of the drill bits we use on smaller drills for projects around the house.

A four- or five-person crew works the machinery, called a drilling rig. They are supervised by a person called a driller. Another worker, known as

Workers check an oil drill bit on a rig in Oman.

the derrick operator, works on a platform high above the drill floor. Other people, nicknamed roughnecks, work on the drill floor below the derrick operator. Together, they begin drilling the well, a process called spudding in.

Companies don't just drill down, or vertically. They also drill at angles and horizontally. They even make branches from one hole to another. This

is known as directional drilling. Directional drilling helps oil companies reduce the number of wells (and the surface area) needed to recover petroleum. This helps them meet today's environmental standards.

When workers hit petroleum, the original pipe that was part of the drilling process now comes out of the hole. Lengths of metal pipe, or casing, replace it. Cement is pumped into the gap outside the casing to reinforce the sides of the hole. A pipe system is installed that connects the new oil well to storage tanks. Underground pressure often forces the petroleum through the pipes. But sometimes workers use pumps or send down water, steam, or gas to help force the petroleum upward.

The petroleum still isn't of much use at this point. The next step is to transport it to factories where it is turned into products such as gasoline.

CHAPTER THREE

PIPELINES AND SUPERTANKERS

Oil pipes are ready to be used at a drilling site in southern Pakistan.

Matthew kept watching the pumpjacks as the car pulled back onto the road. "So what do the workers do after they find a new well?" he asked.

"Go somewhere else and look for more," Uncle John said. "The world always needs more petroleum. Companies are finding it in new places all the time. Not just in the United States, but in Central Asia, and in Africa, in the Arctic. Now you know how much work it takes to find the very best spots to drill."

"If petroleum comes from all those places, though, how does it get here?"

Uncle John turned onto another road. Tall metal towers rose in the distance. "That takes a lot of work, too," he answered.

Tanker trucks deliver gasoline to gas stations.

✳ ✳ ✳

Gasoline moves along a **supply chain**. A supply chain is a system that connects those who mine, log, or otherwise acquire a raw material to the people who want to buy the products made from it. When it comes to gasoline, the supply chain begins on the oil field, with the driller and his crew bringing petroleum out of the ground. The next step is to start moving it on its way to the consumer.

The Trans-Alaska Pipeline crosses three mountain ranges and hundreds of rivers and streams.

On March 27, 1975, workers began to build the Trans-Alaska Pipeline System. The $8 billion project linked the massive petroleum field at Prudhoe Bay, on the Arctic Ocean, with Valdez, a port on Alaska's southern coast. The pipeline opened 2½ years later. Between 1977 and 2005, it transported 15 billion **barrels** of petroleum from the Arctic to waiting ships at Valdez. The Trans-Alaska Pipeline System is just one of many pipelines. There are 33,000 miles (53,108 km) of pipeline in the Gulf of

21st Century Content

The government of Saudi Arabia owns Saudi Aramco, the largest of the world's petroleum corporations. Formed after World War II, the corporation started out as the Arabian-American Oil Company, an alliance between the Saudi king, Ibn Saud, and four American companies. The Saudis had the petroleum. The Americans supplied the machinery and built roads, power plants, and the wells to draw both water and crude oil.

As the 1980s began, the Saudi government bought out the American companies and took control of Aramco. The company name became Saudi Aramco in 1988. Today, Aramco controls almost all of Saudi Arabia's petroleum, natural gas, and related resources. More than 8 million barrels of petroleum flow out of Aramco wells and facilities every day.

Mexico and 166,000 miles (267,151 km) of oil pipeline in the contiguous United States.

The United States gets about half of its petroleum from the Western Hemisphere. About 17 percent of it originates in the nations surrounding the Persian Gulf. Saudi Arabia, for example, controls the Ghawar petroleum field, the largest in history. This oil field has been the source of more than 80 billion barrels of crude oil since its discovery in 1948.

Pipelines carry Ghawar petroleum to Dhahran, Saudi Arabia, a port on the Persian Gulf. While pipelines work for getting crude oil across land, it still needs to be carried to the factories that turn it into gasoline. For that task, companies turn to an important kind of ship called an oil tanker and its giant cousin, the supertanker.

Supertankers are more than 1,000 feet (305 m) long. Some of them would tower as high as, or higher than, the Empire State

A tanker is filled with crude oil in Kuwait. It must pass through the Strait of Hormuz to get to the Indian Ocean.

Building if stood on one end. Though enormous, the ships require crews of only 20 or 30 people, with a handful of officers. Throughout the journey, the crewmen do maintenance, monitor the weather, and bicycle around the ship to solve any problems that come up.

Supertankers heading out of Persian Gulf ports like Dhahran must pass through the Strait of Hormuz. This important waterway passes between Iran and Oman. Ships going in both directions squeeze through an area about 6 miles (9.7 km) wide. The route is considered so important

Because petroleum generates money, many nations have developed industries to extract and sell it. Twelve of the largest producers belong to the Organization of Petroleum Exporting Countries (OPEC). OPEC members cooperate on the amount of petroleum produced and, to some extent, on the prices to be charged. These countries—Saudi Arabia, Iran, Iraq, Kuwait, Qatar, the United Arab Emirates, Libya, Algeria, Nigeria, Angola, Indonesia, and Venezuela—produce approximately 40 percent of the world's crude oil.

Why do you think leaders organized OPEC? What are the advantages for its member countries?

that U.S. warships sometimes patrol there to guarantee the petroleum gets through.

Crude oil prices change by the minute. Traders may buy and sell the petroleum on a tanker once or many times during a ship's journey. Many factors influence the price. A war in an oil-producing country or a terrorist attack on a pipeline may cause prices to rise sharply because of worries that supplies may fall off. On the other hand, stable conditions and good news encourage lower prices. As a result, the petroleum hauled by a tanker may be worth much more or much less by the time the ship reaches port.

A tanker nearing land prepares to pump the crude oil into a new pipeline system. These pipes lead to a refinery, the factory that transforms petroleum into gasoline. This is the next link in the supply chain.

CHAPTER FOUR

THE REFINERY

Tanker ships transport oil around the world.

Uncle John pulled off the road again. Matthew could see towers with staircases spiraling around them. Other towers were topped by flickering flames. Huge tanks nearby were in need of a paint job. He also saw what looked like a thousand miles of pipes—climbing pipes and elbow pipes and straight stretches of pipe as long as a football field. A few workers walked around in coveralls, hard hats, and goggles.

Crude oil is turned into gasoline and other fuels at refineries.

"This is the refinery where I work," his uncle said.

"It's huge!" said Matthew.

"It is about the size of a small town," Uncle John said. "It even has its own fire department and hospital."

"This is where they turn the petroleum into gasoline?" Matthew asked.

"Yep," Uncle John said. "A lot of other products, too. Kerosene, jet fuel, diesel fuel for big trucks. Actually, a lot of products come out of a barrel of crude oil. But gasoline is a high priority. That's where the money is."

There are 149 refineries in the United States. Many states have at least one, but the Gulf Coast is the center for the industry. The facility run by oil giant ExxonMobil at Baytown, Texas, ranks as the country's largest. It processes more than 550,000 barrels of crude oil per day. But it is not the world's largest refinery. Venezuela's Paraguana Refinery in Punto Fijo currently processes the most petroleum of any refinery in the world—more than 900,000 barrels per day.

Refining starts with a process called **separation**. High-pressure steam heats the petroleum to more than 1,000 degrees Fahrenheit (538 degrees Celsius), which turns it into vapor and liquid. The vapor then flows into a distillation tower. Trays with holes or loose caps sit at different levels inside the tower. Temperatures are highest at the bottom, coolest at the top.

Several different substances float in the petroleum vapor. Each settles on the trays at different heights in the tower, depending on its boiling point. Gasoline, a light substance with a low boiling point, floats to the top, where it will turn into a liquid. Liquid petroleum gas, even lighter

than gasoline, rises to the very top. Medium-heavy components like kerosene and diesel fuel settle in the middle. At the bottom are thick and heavy substances that go into making asphalt and other products.

Further refining, or **conversion**, allows a company to turn some of the other components into gasoline. Refiners do this by "cracking" apart the heavier kinds of molecules with 1,000° F (538° C) heat and high pressure. As the molecules break up, they become lighter and smaller, like gasoline. Cracking takes a lot of machinery—a large reactor and a system of furnaces, just for starters. But it's worth it. Turning less-valuable components into very valuable gasoline makes a barrel of oil more profitable for the refiner.

Before it is sold, gasoline is treated by taking out impurities and adding chemicals. The type of treatment determines if gasoline is "regular unleaded" or "premium," among other things. Refiners can also tinker with how the gas will burn

Asphalt is a petroleum product that is used for paving roads.

in a car to make it work better at high altitudes or produce less pollution. For example, BP's Carson Refinery near Los Angeles, California, specializes in making a low-pollution gasoline required by California law.

CHAPTER FIVE

FILL 'ER UP

In the 1960s, attendants still pumped gas for customers at most gas stations.

By the time they returned from the refinery, the fuel gauge on Uncle John's car was close to empty. He pulled in under the canopy of a gas station. Matthew watched as his uncle put a credit card into the pump, waited, and then shoved the nozzle into the car's gas tank.

"I remember when Grandpa used to tell me stories about when he was a kid," Uncle John said. "He told me that other people used to pump the gas for you at gas stations."

"Why?" Matthew asked.

"Because it was their job. Grandpa did it during the summer when he was in high school. People pulled in, and he offered to check their oil and wash the windows while the gas was pumping."

"That's better than pumping your own gas!" Matthew exclaimed.

"Well, it sounds better," Uncle John said. "But the self-serve stations took over because gas there cost less. You see, at a self-serve station the owner didn't have to pay employees, so he could take a few cents off the price of gas. People figured it was worth it to pump their own if they got a better price. Pretty soon, most gas stations were self-serve."

Matthew watched the numbers on the pump. The amount after the dollar sign added up fast. As he wondered how the gas got from the refinery to the station, Uncle John resumed his story.

✳ ✳ ✳

Refineries pump gasoline through pipelines to the next link in the supply chain: the giant, drum-shaped tanks at a **bulk storage terminal**. Gasoline belonging to different companies flows into the tanks. Before it is pumped into the trucks, however, a package of chemical additives goes into it. Each company—whether it's ExxonMobil, Shell, Chevron, or British Petroleum—uses its own recipe. This is what really makes one brand of gasoline different from another.

Many people use credit cards to pay for their gasoline.

Truck drivers line up at the bulk storage terminal to load up their trucks. They pay for the gasoline with a plastic card similar to a credit card. Now the fuel belongs to whatever company employs them.

Tanker trucks carry the fuel in tanks that hold more than 4,000 gallons (15,142 l) of liquid. Many trucks pull two tanks. Since the truck tank is built with separate compartments, a tanker can carry more than one product. For example, regular unleaded gasoline might be in one compartment and premium gasoline in another.

A schedule determines when and where the tanker makes its deliveries. Drivers across the country make about 50,000 deliveries per day. They have to obey a strict set of rules. For example, they cannot go over the speed limit, no matter what. A driver who gets two speeding tickets is fined and suspended from work for six months. Employers even track their drivers with satellite systems to monitor their speed.

Gas stations have underground tanks that hold the different kinds of gasoline. The truck driver pumps whatever products he's carrying into each tank through a hose. Once finished, he heads off to his next delivery, or back to a terminal for another load. Or he might clean the inside of the tank.

Meanwhile, customers cruise past the gas stations, comparing their prices. The price can and often does change daily as petroleum prices fluctuate. In late summer of 2005, Hurricane Katrina interrupted petroleum shipments and forced Gulf Coast refineries to cut back or shut down. The uncertainty over supplies caused prices to go sky-high. Some stations changed their prices two or three times a day to keep up.

What comes out of the gas pump down the street may have come out of the ground thousands of miles away—in Saudi Arabia or Venezuela or northern Alaska. Gasoline makes the global economy go.

21st Century Content

Gas stations have been around since 1907. Years ago, petroleum companies like Texaco and Shell built stations that displayed their distinctive **corporate logos**. They came up with all kinds of gimmicks to make drivers loyal to their brand of gas. Attendants dressed in special uniforms. They offered to clean your windows and check your oil while your gas tank was being filled. Signs advertised clean bathrooms. Station owners drew customers inside by selling cold drinks and candy. In fact, today's stations often make more profit from selling products such as soda and bottled water than they do from gasoline.

Today's gas stations are different from gas stations of many years ago. What do you think brought about the changes?

This map shows the countries and cities mentioned in the text.

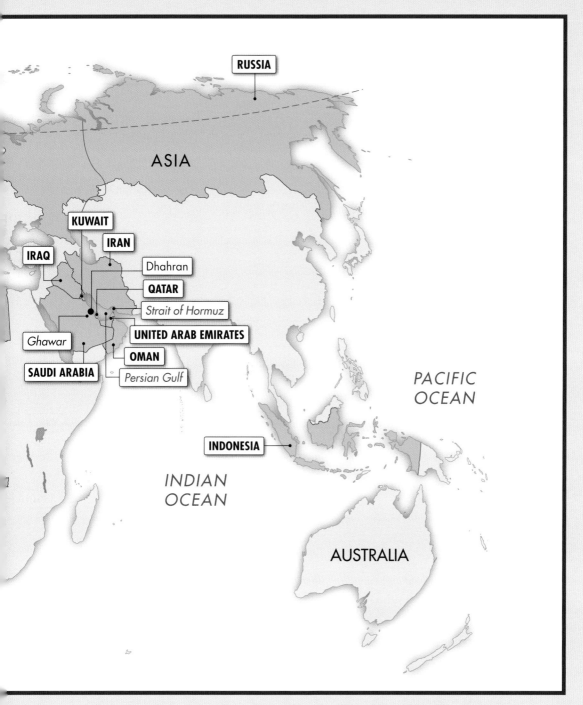

RUSSIA

ASIA

KUWAIT

IRAN

IRAQ

Dhahran

QATAR

Strait of Hormuz

UNITED ARAB EMIRATES

Ghawar

OMAN

SAUDI ARABIA

Persian Gulf

INDONESIA

PACIFIC OCEAN

INDIAN OCEAN

AUSTRALIA

They are the locations of some of the companies involved in making and selling of gasoline.

GLOSSARY

barrels (BEHR-uhlz) a term used by the petroleum industry as a unit of measurement; one barrel of petroleum equals 42 gallons

bit (BIT) the tool on the end of a drillpipe used to cut and crush rock while drilling

bulk storage terminal (BUHLK STOR-ij TUR-muh-nuhl) where refined gasoline bound for gas stations is stored

conversion (kuhn-VER-shuhn) the process of turning less-desirable components of petroleum into more valuable gasoline

corporate logos (KOR-puh-rut LOW-goz) symbols that companies use to mark their products for easy recognition by consumers. The Nike "swoosh" and the red cross of the American Red Cross are two well-known logos.

kerosene (KER-uh-seen) a petroleum product used for lamps and fuel. Before electricity, kerosene lamps were an important source of light.

pipeline (PIPE-line) a series of linked pipes that transport gasoline and other petroleum products

raw material (RAW muh-TIHR-ee-uhl) an unprocessed or partially processed substance that serves as the basis of one or many products. Petroleum provides the raw material for gasoline.

separation (sep-uh-RAY-shuhn) a process that turns petroleum into steam and liquid and separates it into several components, including gasoline

supply chain (suh-PLYE CHAYN) a system that connects raw materials to manufacturers and then to people who wish to buy a finished product made from those materials

FOR MORE INFORMATION

Books

Farndon, John. *Oil*. New York: Dorling Kindersley, 2007.

Laughlin, Rosemary. *John D. Rockefeller: Oil Baron and Philanthropist*. Greensboro, NC: Morgan Reynolds, 2004.

Sutherland, Jonathan, and Diane Canwell. *Container Ships and Oil Tankers*. Pleasantville, NY: Gareth Stevens, 2007.

Zronik, John Paul. *Oil and Gas*. New York: Crabtree Publishing, 2004.

Web Sites

California Energy Commission—What's in a Barrel of Oil?
www.energy.ca.gov/gasoline/whats_in_barrel_oil.html
Find out what can be made from one barrel of crude oil

Energy Information Administration Energy Kid's Page—Petroleum (Oil): A Fossil Fuel
www.eia.doe.gov/kids/energyfacts/sources/non-renewable/oil.html
Information about how petroleum was formed and the products made from it

Energy Information Administration Energy Kids's Page—Petroleum Timeline
www.eia.doe.gov/kids/history/timelines/petroleum.html
Read about the history of petroleum from 3000 B.C. to today

INDEX

ABOUT THE AUTHOR

Kevin Cunningham is the author of several books, including biographies of Joseph Stalin and J. Edgar Hoover and a series on diseases in human history. He lives in Chicago.